D0498468

WISDOM OF THE HEART

OTHER HAY HOUSE LIFESTYLES TITLES OF RELATED INTEREST

Books

10 Secrets for Success and Inner Peace,
by Dr. Wayne W. Dyer

Inner Wisdom, by Louise L. Hay

Interpreting Dreams A–Z, by Leon Nacson

A Journal of Love and Healing,
by Sylvia Browne and Nancy Dufresne

Little Things Make a Big Difference, by Laurin Sydney

The Love and Power Journal, by Lynn V. Andrews

Meditations, by Sylvia Browne

Pleasant Dreams, by Amy E. Dean

Simple Things, by Jim Brickman

Card Decks

The Four Agreements Cards, by DON Miguel Ruiz

Healing with the Fairies Oracle Cards
(booklet and card deck), by Doreen Virtue, Ph.D.

If Life Is a Game, These Are the Rules Cards,
by Chérie Carter-Scott, Ph.D.

Inner Peace Cards, by Dr. Wayne W. Dyer

MarsVenus Cards, by John Gray

Self-Care Cards, by Cheryl Richardson

Wisdom Cards, by Louise L. Hay

Zen Cards, by Daniel Levin

All of the above titles may be ordered by calling
Hay House at: (760) 431-7695 or (800) 654-5126
(760) 431-6948 (fax) or (800) 650-5115 (fax)
www.hayhouse.com

WISDOM OF THE HEART

INSPIRATION FOR A LIFE WORTH LIVING

Alan Cohen

Hay House, Inc.
Carlsbad, California • Sydney, Australia
Canada • Hong Kong • United Kingdom

Published and distributed in the United States by: Hay House, Inc., P.O. Box 5100, Carlsbad, CA 92018-5100 • (800) 654-5126 • (800) 650-5115 (fax) • www.hayhouse.com • ***Published and distributed in Australia by:*** Hay House Australia Pty Ltd, P.O. Box 515, Brighton-Le-Sands, NSW 2216 *phone:* 1800 023 516 • *e-mail:* info@hayhouse.com.au • ***Distributed in the United Kingdom by:*** Airlift, 8 The Arena, Mollison Ave., Enfield, Middlesex, United Kingdom EN3 7NL • ***Distributed in Canada by:*** Raincoast, 9050 Shaughnessy St., Vancouver, B.C., Canada V6P 6E5

Editorial supervision: Jill Kramer
Cover and interior design: Ashley Brown

Library of Congress Cataloging-in-Publication Data

Cohen, Alan
Wisdom of the heart : inspiration for a life worth living / Alan Cohen.
p. cm.
Includes bibliographical references.
ISBN 1-56170-952-2 (hardcover)
1. Spiritual life. I. Title.

BL624 .C596 2002
291.4'32—dc21

2002003493

ISBN 1-56170-952-2

05 04 03 02 4 3 2 1
1st printing, October 2002

Printed in China

Contents

INTRODUCTION

As you navigate through the adventure of life, you'll probably look to many sources for guidance. When you seek answers from external authorities, however, you may become overwhelmed and confused. You'll find a deluge of information, when what you really need is inspiration. So where can you turn for answers that will satisfy you?

For thousands of years, sages and seers have encouraged us to look within our own hearts for the truth we seek. Intellectual knowledge goes just so far—it helps, but ultimately we yearn for deeper knowing. Because we're spiritual beings, nothing less than spiritual answers will fulfill us.

Wisdom of the Heart brings you a treasure trove of illumination and direction. Here you'll find a wealth of stories, poems, parables, profound quotations, and humorous quips from a wide variety of sources. Over many years of studying and teaching self-development, I've read and heard many thousands of anecdotes and wise insights. These are my favorites, the ones I keep coming back to for inspiration—for myself, my readers, and my students.

Each chapter in this book begins with a story or poetic quotation. I then provide commentary upon the selection, which expands upon its message. All of the selections highlight principles upon which you can build a rewarding life, and they can help you move through significant transitions that you may encounter on your journey.

It's no accident that there are 52 selections in this book, for I invite you to savor each passage for a week. Let the message sink into your mind and heart until it becomes a part of you. Rather than skimming through the stories as you would a magazine, take one at a time and absorb it like a glass of fine wine or a piece of rich chocolate. Bathe in its meaning, and then put the book aside. Adopt the theme for your week, and then move on to the next passage and be with that one. Reading these words is one thing; living them makes them real in your experiences. Enjoy what unfolds over the next year!

If you're a teacher, counselor, minister, or health professional, feel free to use this material in your presentations and interactions. Inspiration only increases as it is shared, and then everyone gains.

Blessings on your great adventure! May you recognize the wisdom in your own heart, and bring it to life more and more every day.

I

Great and Noble Things

My child, in the life ahead of you, keep your capacity for faith and belief, but let your judgment watch what you believe. Keep your love of life, but throw away your fear of death. Life must be loved or it is lost. . . . Keep your wonder at great and noble things, like sunlight and thunder, the rain and the stars, and the greatness of heroes. Keep your heart hungry for new knowledge. Keep your hatred of a lie, and keep your power of indignation. . . . I am ashamed to leave you in an uncomfortable world, but someday it will be better. And when that day comes, you will thank God for the greatest blessing man can receive: living in peace.

— letter from a Yugoslav soldier in
World War II to his unborn child
(the man was later executed)

We all want to leave our children a better world than the one we found. The greatest legacy you can bestow is joy, which is a choice you can make right now. If you wait until the world changes to let your light shine, your dream will wither and die. Make your joy conditional on *nothing* outside you and on *everything* inside you. Then your children will have a role model of self-generated happiness.

Life is a game of focusing your attention. Everything you can imagine is out there. You'll never eliminate all the things you don't like or wish would go away, and resistance only creates more of what you fight against. To claim the life you desire, devote your mind, heart, and energy to everything you love, and let the rest be. Life is too precious to waste on what you don't want—but it's fully worth focusing on everything you *do* want.

Wonder and appreciation lift us up beyond the mundane. Do whatever it takes to find and create magic in your life. Bathe in the light of the full moon; gaze into a star-jeweled night; let yourself be lulled to sleep by the rhythm of waves. Life is seeking to love you. Are you letting it?

Sing Your Song

When a woman in a certain African tribe knows she's pregnant, she goes out into the wilderness with a few friends. Together they pray and meditate until they hear the baby's unique song. As they attune to it, the women sing it aloud. Then they return to the tribe and teach it to everyone else.

When the child is born, the community gathers and sings the child's song to them. When the child enters school, the villagers gather and sing the song. When the child passes through the initiation to adulthood, the people again come together and sing. At the altar of marriage, the person hears their song. Finally, when it's time for the soul to pass from this world, the family and friends gather at the person's bed, just as they did at their birth, and they sing the person to the next life.

There is one other occasion upon which the villagers sing to the child. If, at any time during the person's life, they commit a crime or socially aberrant act, they're called to the center of the village. There the people in the community form a circle around the person and sing their song to them.

A friend is someone who knows your song and sings it to you when you've forgotten it yourself.

Your soul has its own song. Your unique energy and purpose are expressed through your talents, passions, and visions. When you're in touch with your joy and act upon it, your heart feels full and your life is rewarding. When you're disconnected from your passion, you feel empty, your life is frustrating, and you wonder what you're doing here.

Yet even when you're distracted by the fears and troubles of the world, your song still lives inside you. Its tune is etched upon your soul more deeply than any experience could be. As you move through difficulties, detours, or setbacks, your spirit guides you from within, urging you to carry on and emerge shining. In the face of a great challenge, your inner knowing comes forth in unprecedented power. All of your life lessons help you get back in touch with the music of your soul.

Others may try to influence you to sing *their* song rather than yours. If you do, you'll become resentful and lose your voice. To regain it, get back in touch with your truth and act on it. Never deny your expression for another's. You can harmonize and support someone else, but don't do it at the expense of your own happiness.

You best serve others by reminding them of their song. Judgment, punishment, and power plays don't correct; they only drive human beings further from their joy and aggravate pain and self-defeating behavior. When someone is in distress or conflict, help them remember who they really are, and they'll have no need to hurt others.

Authentic self-expression brings healing, release, and relief. Remember your song, and you'll become magnetic and compelling . . . you'll also find peace within yourself.

3

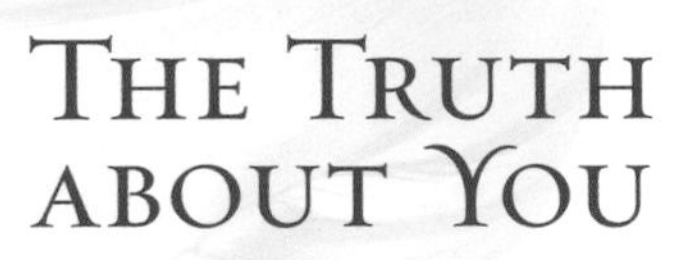

The Truth about You

Dear God,

please help me

to recognize

the truth about

myself, no matter

how beautiful

it is.

Fearful minds have taught you that the truth about yourself is so horrid that you couldn't handle what you'd find if you dared to look. Yet, in reality, your truth is so magnificent that if you *did* look upon it, you'd find validation and inspiration to be all that you have the potential to be.

Most of what you think about yourself is learned from outside opinions. You've adopted dark self-images that have been projected onto you by others who don't know or love *themselves*. You began to believe that you were deficient or evil, to the point that whenever attention was drawn to your inner self, you cringed in fear of being exposed. But the best thing that could ever happen to your true self would be to expose it, for it's sparkling and wonderful in every way. It's really who God created you to be.

If you fear looking at your true self, you'll find many ways to distract yourself from it. Busyness, drama, and addictions are ways of avoiding facing yourself. To find the peace you seek, stop running and just *be*. Get to know who you really are. Remember the wholeness you felt before you joined the rush to nowhere. Then you'll recognize yourself through the eyes of love, and everything will be different.

Your Passionate Purpose

I would rather be ashes than dust!
I would rather that my spark should
burn out in a brilliant blaze than
it should be stifled by dry rot.
I would rather be a superb
meteor, every atom of me in
magnificent glow, than a sleepy
and permanent planet.
The function of man is to live,
not to exist. I shall not waste
my days in trying to prolong them.
I shall use my time.

— Jack London

The purpose of life isn't to safely arrive at death—it's to live so well that when death comes, you don't even notice it. You just go from life to greater life.

Most people spend a great deal of time and energy protecting themselves from the things they fear. As a result, they don't really *live;* they merely *survive.* In denying their dreams, they sell themselves and their lives short. Life isn't about pedaling faster to keep up; it's about soaring beyond the limits you've been taught to have.

When you come to the end of your journey, it won't be what you *did* that will cause you regret—it will be what you *didn't* do. Don't compromise your adventure. Bring your passion to life, and life will bring your passion to you.

Passion is the voice of God calling you to awaken to your true purpose. When you follow your heart and pursue your unique path, you live from *inspiration*, not *desperation.* Stay true to your passion, and death will never be able to touch you. If you celebrate your heart's desires, you'll deliver life to everyone you touch.

Caller I.D.

At 9:00 P.M. on June 4, 2000, Lorenzo was relaxing at his home in Hawaii when the telephone rang. When he answered, a woman's voice on the other end asked, "Who is this?"

"This is Lorenzo. How can I help you?"

"Well, your phone number is on my caller I.D., and I wanted to know why you called me," the woman answered.

"Who is this?"

"My name is Michelle—from Utah."

"I didn't call you. I don't know any Michelles in Utah."

"Well, you had to have called me, because your number and your name are right in front of me: 'Lorenzo . . . 808 . . .'"

Lorenzo thought for a moment and said, "I've got it! I must have been calling one of my friends in Utah, and accidentally dialed your number." He read her the telephone numbers of his two friends who lived in Utah . . . they weren't even in the same area code. Lorenzo was stumped. "I just don't have an explanation for this—but I definitely didn't call you," he reiterated.

As the two kept talking, Lorenzo found that he was attracted to Michelle's voice and spunkiness. She wasn't going to get off the phone until she found out why he called her.

After a while, Lorenzo blurted out without thinking, "Well, Michelle, I will tell you one thing: If we ever get married, this will make a great story."

She laughed, and they continued to talk for almost two hours. And then they talked every night, with some of the calls lasting six hours.

A few days after his original call from Michelle, Lorenzo called his friend Steve in Utah, and the mystery was unraveled. Steve had purchased three telephones at an electronics store in Salt Lake City and had taken them home to decide which one he liked best. During that time, Lorenzo had phoned him, and his number had registered on the Caller I.D. The next morning, Steve returned the phone to the store. Michelle went to the same store later that day to return a defective phone she'd purchased a week earlier. The salesman told her that they didn't have any other phones like the one she was bringing back, except for one that had just been returned. He asked Michelle if she wanted to wait two to three weeks for a brand-new one to come in or if she wanted the one on hand. She chose the one that had been returned.

When Michelle came home from work the next day, she looked on her Caller I.D. list to see who had called. When she saw the 808 area code and Lorenzo's name, she realized that she didn't know where 808 was, so she decided to call the operator to find out. Somehow when she pressed "O," instead of dialing the operator, the call was put through to Lorenzo.

On September 29, 2000, Lorenzo and Michelle were married on a beach in Hawaii. And yes, they do have a great story to tell.

The universe has amazing ways to bring people together for all the right reasons. While many folks struggle and go to great lengths to find the right apartment, job, or mate, there's an organization working behind the scenes to create perfect connections for us: the CCCC, or the *Cosmic Coincidence Control Center.*

There are no accidents—coincidences are just miracles in which God wishes to remain anonymous. Chance plays no part in God's plan. Everything and everyone who shows up in your life comes at the invitation of your thoughts and intentions.

Lorenzo's "chance" (and in some ways inexplicable) meeting with Michelle represents the culmination of a great momentum of experience, desire, and intention on both of their parts. They were both ripe, ready, and willing to meet a mate, and the Law of Attraction assisted them in playing out their wishes.

If you're trying to manifest something that your heart deeply desires, know that the universe is aware of your intentions and is working to arrange your results. Every strong intention you hold is registered on the Big Caller I.D., and God knows your address. Do what you can on your own behalf without struggle or strain, and leave the details to the CCCC. The more you anxiously try to make something happen, the more you're affirming that you have to do it all yourself. Some of the greatest manifestations have occurred after people have set a ball of intention in motion and then trusted an intelligent yet unseen force to assist them. Pray, intend, visualize, act . . . and then let go. The release is as important as the conjuring.

Regard everyone you meet as a purposeful character in the movie you've scripted. Then keep fine-tuning your script so your movie becomes only better. After all, central casting is on *your* payroll.

Right Before You

A spiritual seeker heard about a holy man who lived in a house atop a remote mountain. It was said that spending even a few minutes in this sage's presence could change a person's life forever.

Hungry for awakening, the seeker dropped everything and set out on a pilgrimage to find this enlightened being and share a few meaningful moments with him. For months he traversed over mountains and through valleys and rivers to find the guru. Finally he arrived at the holy man's front door.

A servant greeted the seeker, ushered him into the house, and guided him through several rooms. Since the fellow was so anxious to meet the guru, he hardly heard a word the servant was saying. After a few minutes, the servant led him to another door, which opened to the backyard. The servant indicated that it was time for him to leave.

"But I was hoping to have a few minutes with the holy man!" cried the disappointed and frustrated seeker.

"You just did," answered the holy man as he closed the door.

If you're preoccupied with seeking, you'll never find what you're looking for. Your answers don't await you on a remote mountaintop—they're right where you are.

God isn't an old man with a white beard sitting on a distant cloud, tossing gumdrops to a lucky few and hurling lightning bolts at everybody else. God lives in your heart and speaks to you through your intuition, visions, and dreams. God isn't a person; God is an energy, a truth that's expressed through all living beings. God isn't contained in one religion or philosophy; God lives in *all* religions . . . and beyond them.

Take care not to become a professional seeker. If you identify yourself as such, you'll just keep searching, like a radio that constantly scans without ever stopping on any one station. You can read thousands of books, attend hundreds of seminars, ask endless questions, engage in lifelong therapy, and still find yourself wondering who you're supposed to be when you grow up.

Seeking is fine, but finding is finer. When you're ready to find rather than seek, your answers will show up everywhere. God will speak to you through a majestic sunrise, the touch of your beloved, and the sparkling eyes of a child. When you recognize that God expresses through the entire world, perfection will no longer elude you—you'll discover it everywhere you look.

By the same token, salvation doesn't rest in the hands of inaccessible authority figures—it shows up in the humble people you encounter in the course of your daily life. Every person you meet is God in a new and fascinating form, each with a unique lesson to teach.

All that you seek is right here . . . in you. All that you seek *is* you.

CREATE A MASTERPIECE

A mother took her young son to a concert by the famous Polish pianist Ignace Jan Paderewski to try to heighten her son's interest in his piano lessons. After they were seated, the mother spotted a friend in the audience and walked down the aisle to greet her.

Seizing the opportunity to investigate the wonders of the concert hall, the little boy rose and eventually made his way through a door marked "No Admittance."

When the house lights dimmed and the concert was about to begin, the mother returned to her seat and discovered that her son was missing.

Suddenly the curtains parted and spotlights focused on the impressive Steinway onstage. In horror, the mother saw her little boy sitting at the keyboard, innocently plinking out "Twinkle, Twinkle, Little Star."

At that moment, the great piano master made his entrance, quickly moved to the piano, and whispered in the boy's ear, "Don't quit. Keep playing." Then, leaning over, Paderewski began filling in the bass part with his left hand.

Soon his right arm reached around to the other side of the child, and Paderewski added a running obbligato. Together, the old master and the young novice transformed a potentially embarrassing situation into a wonderfully creative experience. And the audience was mesmerized.

Often what goes very wrong is the beginning of something going very right; what starts out as a mistake can be turned into a miracle. A visionary sees beyond appearances and thrives under all conditions. People with broader vision aren't subject to conditions—they create them.

A true master can turn anything into a masterpiece. Ingenious people remain open to possibilities beyond the familiar and let their good find them rather than trying to squeeze it out of life. Many significant inventions and medicines were discovered "by accident" while experimenters were trying to develop something quite unrelated.

You can't get rid of negatives by forcing, resisting, or denying; instead, find a way to turn them into positives. Take the raw materials before you and lift them to their highest potential. Act as William Blake suggested when he wrote, "To see a world in a grain of sand / And a heaven in a wild flower / Hold infinity in the palm of your hand / And eternity in an hour."

If you're faced with an awkward situation, step back and see if there's something helpful or playful you can make out of it. You're bigger than any event you encounter—there's a way you can make it work in your favor.

From the perspective of the child in this story, we find a powerful lesson: Paderewski's advice—*"Don't quit; keep playing"*—teaches us to never give up. Even if your skills are rudimentary or clumsy, if you persevere, you'll eventually join in a great symphony. Your efforts will be met by God's compassion, and together you'll create a masterpiece.

Lasting Impact

Name two gold-medal winners
in the 2000 Olympics.
Name four recipients of the Pulitzer Prize.
Name one coach in the NFL Hall of Fame.
Name one person who received the
Congressional Medal of Honor last year.

Name two teachers who made a
significant impact on your life.
Name four authors, poets, or musicians
who have written something you cherish.
Name a coach who taught you
values, discipline, or persistence.
Name one person who would
stand by you in your darkest hour.

Which group has had the most
lasting impact on your life?

While many people receive public accolades, many more deliver priceless gifts in the unsung world of friendship, family, and mentorship. We may celebrate those who impress the masses, but in the long run, those who affect our personal lives make the greater difference in our destiny.

Our daily lives are replete with often-unnoticed heroes who simply help people where they can. You may not read about them in the newspaper and they may never receive prestigious awards, but still they shine like rare jewels. They bring beauty and comfort to everyone they touch by transforming the world from within it. Their real reward isn't money or glory; it's the personal satisfaction of knowing that they gave of themselves in ways that were needed.

Put aside ambition for public recognition, and simply do what you do *because it feels good inside*. If the world applauds you, that's icing on the cake. But no matter what the external response, your inner world will glow with a rare and sacred light . . . along with the lives of those you bless.

Where Wisdom Lives

When the great inventor Thomas Edison felt stymied in the midst of a difficult experiment, he used a unique method to access his answers: He would lie down on a couch with a rock in his hand and take a nap. As he dozed off, he sank into his subconscious mind, which he recognized to be the well-spring of his best ideas and an avenue to infinite intelligence. Then, as his body relaxed, Edison would naturally let loose of his hold on the rock, which would drop to the floor with a loud thud and startle him out of his nap. At that moment, Edison still had fresh in mind the idea he'd unearthed in his sleep state, and he would quickly write it down. That was his secret.

Thomas Edison went on to generate more than 1,000 patents, including those for the incandescent lamp, the phonograph, the alkaline battery, and motion pictures.

There's a place inside of you that already knows your answers. Below and beyond your surface or thinking mind is your superconscious, which is always in direct communication with the mind of God. It *is* the mind of God, which is expressing through you.

You have easy access to your inner genius. Simply remove your focus from your mental chatter, and your inner knowing will emerge. You can tap in to it through many different avenues. One is through deep relaxation: A good night's sleep or solid catnap will clear the slate and allow pure understanding to shine forth. Meditation can open a pipeline to higher awareness. Many people also access their intuition through music, art, dance, creative writing, or an absorbing hobby. Others get to it through vigorous exercise such as running, weight training, or sports. Yoga, tai chi, and martial arts provide additional routes to the same destination. Still others find their connection through nature, allowing God to speak to them through the splendor of primal creation.

No matter how you access wisdom, it's right there, waiting for you at all times. The thinking mind can be helpful, but it's flighty and easily distracted. Real knowing resides within you. When you invite it to come forth, it gladly bestows you with the answers you need.

It Could Be Anyone

One night, a mysterious stranger showed up at the door of a run-down monastery, which was operated by a half-dozen old monks who had become spiritually parched. When the monks welcomed the visitor, they noticed an unusual glow about him. Saying nothing, they ushered him to his room.

The next morning, the monks sat with their guest at breakfast, eager to hear his words of wisdom. "Last night I had a dream," he reported. "It was revealed to me that one of you is the Messiah."

The monks were astonished; in bewilderment, they looked at each other.

"Who is it?" one of them asked.

"That is something I cannot reveal to you," the stranger answered. "You'll have to discover that for yourself." Then, as cryptically as he had arrived, the man departed.

During the weeks and months that followed, the monks treaded lightly with each other and looked into each other's eyes more deeply. They treated each other as if any one of them could be the Messiah.

Then, over a period of time, something miraculous began to happen. For the first time in many years, joy and appreciation began to fill the halls of the monastery. A feeling of eager anticipation enlivened the monks' prayers, meals, and conversations. As a result, people who visited the monastery felt uplifted, and the number of visitors increased. In the course of just a few years, the monastery came back to life, and the order was carried on by new monks who found refreshment for their souls.

Eventually all of the original monks passed on, without any one of them ever being designated as the Messiah. No matter—they had all *become the Messiah.*

If we take our friends and loved ones for granted, we may overlook the extraordinary gifts they bring us. Every person who walks the earth is a god in disguise. Those we celebrate and extol as great spiritual, intellectual, or political leaders are those who see beyond the obvious and call forth the latent greatness in those they touch. If you lift your vision to find the highest in those around you, you'll live in a world of enlightened beings.

Your beliefs and expectations can create saints or monsters. To fan the flame of good in others, treat them as you would like them to be. Expect the best and you'll find it. If you offer others patience, encouragement, and opportunity, they'll step into their magnificence.

Rather than dwelling on the faults of those you encounter, define their greatness as their reality. They will become what you see in them, and your life will become an ever-expanding adventure in drawing forth the best in everyone you meet.

When you find the Messiah in others, you'll find it in yourself as well.

Opportunity!

Around the turn of the 20th century, a shoe manufacturer sent a salesman to Africa to try to expand their market. After a few weeks in the foreign land, the salesman dispatched a telegram to his home office, warning: "Disaster! Disaster! These people don't wear shoes. Cancel production immediately!"

Later that year, a salesman from another shoe manufacturer traveled to the same region, also hoping to increase his company's client base. Soon he sent a telegram to his home office, too. But this one read: "Opportunity! Opportunity! These people don't wear shoes. Triple production immediately!"

Every situation offers you an opportunity—if you're open to recognizing it. Negative thinkers blame their limits or failure on external conditions such as the economy, the weather, germs, incompetent people, politics, childhood programming, cultural conditioning, genetics, reincarnation, karma, and astrological aspects. Yet they rarely look to the one place where limits actually do exist and can be transcended—their own minds.

Obstacles are what you see when you take your eyes off the goal. Complaining about what isn't working only nails you in a box and increases the distance between where you are and where you want to be. A possibility thinker notices a problem just long enough to discover the solution. Success is what you achieve when you give no power to failure.

Success-minded people are service-minded. They realize that there's always a way to help people, and customers are glad to pay for goods and services that improve their lives. In addition, success thinkers recognize that they themselves deserve to be supported for the gifts they render.

Don't be put off by challenges. Each challenge is an illusory limit that exists only to be transcended. With vision and determination, you *will* surmount it. When you hit a wall, it just means that you're being guided to a different door. Your creative genius will map out the route to your dreams.

Spirited Prayer

A priest and a cabdriver arrived
at the Pearly Gates at the same time.
After interviewing them both,
St. Peter opened the Gates and let
the cabdriver into Heaven. Then he told
the priest to have a seat and
await further consideration.
The priest was outraged.
"How can you let that man into
Heaven before me?" he complained.
"I preached every Sunday for
more than 50 years! All this man
did was drive a car around the city!"
"That's right," St. Peter answered.
"When you preached, people slept.
But when this man drove, people prayed."

Spiritual growth has little to do with words and everything to do with experience. We can distract each other—and ourselves—with words and hide behind them. Life experience, however, runs far deeper and stays with us for a longer time.

True prayer isn't a matter of executing a script; it's an intention of the heart. You can utter all the right words, but if your mind is wandering or your intention is weak, you'll reap meager results. If, on the other hand, you reach out for help with sincerity, desire, and faith, you can say few words (or none at all), and your prayer will be answered in a powerful way.

Frightening or challenging experiences move us to ask deeper questions that summon profound answers. They cause us to evaluate how we're living, and remind us of the sacredness of life, our relationships, and our spirit. Suddenly we value things less and people more; we start to manipulate less and respect more. Those who have come close to death have a greater appreciation for life and make more authentic choices.

Put your entire heart into your prayers. And when you're not praying, put your entire heart into your life. Eventually, *all* of your life will become a prayer.

Only Love

Make love now, by night and
by day, in winter and summer . . .
You are in the world for that
and the rest of life is nothing
but vanity, illusion, waste.
There is only one science,
love, one riches, love,
only one policy, love.
To make love is all
the law and the prophets.

— Anatole France

Your life is worthwhile to the extent that you love. True love extends far beyond romance: It embraces love of life, appreciation for each new day, the joy of connecting with beloved friends, celebrating the blessings before you, expressing your unique gifts, enjoying each moment, and so much more.

If you want to find richer meaning and purpose in your life, just keep loving. You won't need guidelines from external sources, for love will give you all the direction that you'll need. Answers will reveal themselves in the right way and time. You'll find wonder and perfection in little things you once overlooked. You'll remember what's important, and your soul will be fulfilled.

The widest gate to the kingdom of love is *appreciation.* Simply find the good in the people and situations around you. Rather than criticizing or defending your foibles and eccentricities, enjoy them, and marvel at the perfection of the universe. Find innocence where others apply judgment, and you'll leave a trail of healing wherever you go.

The secret of life is so simple: *Only love!*

A Look in the Mirror

A traveler approached an ancient city and asked the man sitting by the gate, "What's it like here?"

"What was it like where you came from?" returned the gatekeeper.

"It was an awful place," the traveler answered. "People were unfriendly and ready to take advantage of each other at every turn. There were no jobs and the pollution was horrendous. It was really terrible."

"Well, that's pretty much what you'll find here," answered the gatekeeper. The traveler shook his head and continued on his way.

An hour later, another man approached the gatekeeper and also asked, "What's it like here?"

"What was it like where you came from?" the gatekeeper replied again.

"It was a lovely place—friendly people, beautiful vistas, lots of wonderful food, and rich culture. I felt very blessed to live there."

"Well, that's pretty much what you'll find here," answered the gatekeeper.

The man smiled and walked through the gates to his new home.

We see the world not as it is, but as we are. The reality you experience is the one you carry with you in your mind. Therefore, the vision you use is crucial to your destiny.

All of life is a self-fulfilling prophecy. Your experience isn't created by outside agents, but by your attitudes and beliefs. As a co-creator with God, imbued with free will, you're powerful enough to generate a world in your mind and then step into it in your experience.

If you find yourself repeating negative patterns in your relationships, work, finances, or health, you can be sure that you're holding a self-limiting belief. Rather than cursing events because they're hurting you, bless them as a reflection of your inner thoughts. You can choose to thank everyone who shows up in your life, for they can all teach you about yourself. Don't be fooled into thinking that what they're saying or doing is separate from your own mind. Other people don't really live outside you—they live inside you. Their judgment or attack reflects your own. Change *your* mind, and *they* will also change accordingly.

If you experience rewarding patterns in your life, then you must be holding beliefs founded in self-love and respect. Those who honor and support you are reflecting your knowledge that you're worthy of the good you seek.

The world you live in is one of your own creation, so make it the one you would choose.

Your Inner Bible

The first time I went [to the Magic Monastery] *I forgot to bring my Bible. When I asked the guestmaster if I could borrow a Bible, he said, "Wouldn't you care to write your own?"*

"What do you mean?"

"Well, write your own Bible—something of your own on the order of the Bible. You could tell of a classical bondage and the great liberation, a promised land, sacred songs, a messiah—that kind of thing. Ought to be much more interesting than just reading someone else's Bible. And you might learn more."

Well, I set to work. It took me a month. I never learned so much about the official Bible. When I was finished, he recommended I take it home and try to live according to it for a year. . . . It was quite a year. An eye opener. Most certainly I had never put so much energy and alertness into living my official Bible as I was putting into living this one. And my daily meditations had never been so concentrated.

When I arrived back for my next retreat, [the guestmaster] *greeted me very warmly, took into his hands my Bible and my journal, kissed them with the greatest reverence, and told me I could spend a couple of days and nights in the Hall of the Great Fire. On the last night of the year, I should consign my two books to the flames. That's what I did. A whole year's wisdom and labor—into the Great Fire. Afterwards he set me to writing another Bible.*

And so it went, these past 40 years—each year a new Bible, a new journal, and then at the end of the year—into the flames.

— Theophane the Monk

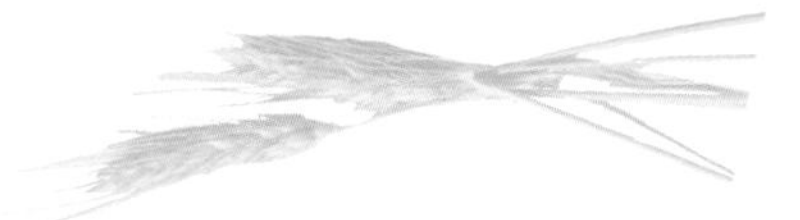

A Bible is a saga of awakening and reconnection to God. Every day you're awakening to new insights and discovering your personal relationship with Spirit. While you're trying to find God, God is trying to find you—and rendezvous you will. That cosmic meeting can occur today or any day, for it's available whenever you choose. You just need to be open to the ways that Spirit is speaking to you through the encounters of your daily life.

All the wisdom you seek in traditional Bibles is contained within your own inner Bible. You'll find that your Bible is even more meaningful to you, for it tells your unique story. Your life is a constantly unfolding epic adventure, filled with colorful characters, plot turns, and amazing surprises. And everything that happens is related to your enlightenment. So your experiences are just as valid as those who found God long ago. These are indeed Biblical times.

God is writing a Bible in your heart—one you can joyfully live by.

The Films You Watch

Paul "Bear" Bryant, the legendary former coach of the University of Alabama Crimson Tide football team, had a secret upon which he built his success: When Bryant showed his team film footage of their previous games, he focused only on the plays they starred in. He didn't show the players films of their mistakes, only their successes. As a result, the Crimson Tide kept winning like no other team.

Bear Bryant led his teams to more college football victories than any other coach in college football history. During his tenure, from 1958 to 1982, the Crimson Tide won an extraordinary 323 games (out of 362 outings) and six national championships, and was selected for bowl games 24 times. He's regarded as one of the greatest coaches of all time—largely because his teams watched the right films.

You cannot succeed by focusing on what went wrong, for whatever you concentrate on becomes the foundation for your next experience. Harping on your errors just sets you up for more of them.

Of course we learn from our mistakes; after all, they're helpful growth experiences. The question isn't whether or not to pay attention to them, but *how much* attention you give to them. Once you realize that you've made an error, extract the lesson and turn your full attention to your desired result. Errors are good stepping-stones to your dreams, but if you keep standing on them, you'll never get where you want to go.

You can't beat yourself into happiness—the only way to become happy is to do the things that make you happy. Celebrating your victories engenders more of the same. Fascination is fertilizer—whatever you pay attention to, grows. Dwell on where you want to go, not where you came from. *Your history is not your destiny.* Hasten your destiny by living *from* it rather than moving toward it.

The films you watch . . . you become.

Relief and Release

When Fiorello La Guardia was mayor of New York City in 1935, he showed up in court one night in the poorest area of New York City and suggested the judge go home for the evening as he took over the bench.

La Guardia's first case involved an elderly woman arrested for stealing bread. When asked whether she was innocent or guilty, she answered softly, "I needed the bread, your honor, to feed my grandchildren."

"I've no option but to punish you," the mayor responded. "Ten dollars or ten days in jail."

Proclaiming the sentence, he simultaneously threw $10 into his hat. He then fined every person in the courtroom 50 cents for living in a city "where a grandmother has to steal food to feed her grandchildren."

When all had contributed their 50 cents, the woman paid her fine and left the courtroom with an additional $47.50.

— recounted by Glenn Van Ekeren

Every encounter is an opportunity to apply judgment or compassion. Judgment calls for punishment, while compassion brings release. You have the power to deliver either. When you inflict pain, you separate yourself from love; when you bestow relief, you become godlike.

Those who commit crimes or engage in antisocial behavior are calling for love. They feel powerless and don't know how to get the love they want, so they try to take it by force. Then they're judged and condemned, which just makes them angrier and more resistant. So the dark cycle is reinforced and continued.

The cycle is broken by seeing beyond appearances. If you can find it in your heart to offer another person forgiveness, relief, and release when they're expecting crucifixion or punishment, you open the door to real and lasting change.

Compassion and forgiveness are gifts you give to yourself, through others. Lead others from a cross to a garden, and you walk with them.

Smoke Signals

A lone shipwreck survivor on an uninhabited island managed to build a rude hut in which he placed all that he had saved. Every day he prayed to God for deliverance and anxiously scanned the horizon in hopes of seeing a passing ship.

One day while he was cooking breakfast in his little house, he saw on the horizon the outline of an ocean liner. Frantically he ran to the beach and jumped up and down excitedly, waving his arms and screaming at the top of his lungs. Alas, the ship just kept going and made no movement in his direction.

Dismayed and dejected, the man turned back to his hut and found that it had caught fire. Within the hour it burned to the ground; all that he had was gone. The man sat on a rock and cried—surely this was the worst day of his life.

The next morning the ship arrived to rescue him. He was elated beyond words. "How did you know I was here?" he asked the captain.

"We saw your smoke signal," the captain answered.

— Adapted from Walter A. Heiby

Never judge an experience on face value alone. Sometimes what seems to be the worst thing that could happen turns out to be the best. A setback is really a setup, and behind every tragedy awaits a gift. If you're open to the gift, it will be revealed.

When you pray or intend for something to happen, don't dictate the form or timing of the results. Instead, pray for the quality of your experience. Pay more attention to how you want to feel than how the outcome looks. You can manifest all the things you pray for but still be unhappy. Instead, pray for happiness, and the building blocks to that happiness will reveal themselves in the right way and time.

When something painful happens, it isn't the end of the story—it's simply another chapter in the book. Hang in there until the end of the tale and you'll find value and meaning in everything that happened, and you'll recognize its role in your awakening.

CELEBRATE!

In the 15th century, a group of ascetic monks spent their entire chaste lives scribing copies of the Bible. One day one of the elderly monks told another, "I think I'll go into our vault and take a look at our earliest copy of the Bible. We've been making copies from copies for many years, and I'd like to reacquaint myself with the original text."

A few hours later, the monk returned. His body was shaking, his eyes were bulging, and he looked as if he had just seen a ghost.

"Brother Theodore!" the other monk cried out. "What did you see in there?"

"It's 'celebrate'!" Brother Theodore exclaimed. "With an 'r.'"

We're not here to fight against ourselves—we're here to celebrate all that God has created us to be. Sexuality and the desires of the body are natural impulses built into the fabric of life by an intelligent Creator. To deny them is to refute life; to allow them to express in a healthy and natural way is to fulfill God's intentions.

We've been taught that our passions are evil, but they're really an avenue for divine expression. The more you try to resist or override physical pleasures, the more power they'll end up having over you, to the point that they'll finally become your ruler. When, on the other hand, you respect your body as a wondrous creation and recognize that God is making love through you, you can then honor and embrace the totality of your being and elevate your sexual and sensual nature as a sacred element of life.

Everything you are is beautiful and good. As Walt Whitman proclaimed, "Welcome is every organ and attribute of me. . . . Not an inch nor a particle of an inch is vile, and none shall be less familiar than the rest." If you're intent on loving yourself, love *all* of yourself. You can practice by standing naked in front of a mirror and releasing your judgments until you truly appreciate what you see. Then you'll see yourself as God knows you.

As you find more and more beauty in yourself, you'll in turn find more and more beauty in the world. One day you'll wake up and realize that the world has been beautiful all along—you just didn't realize it. Then everything you do will be an act of celebration.

The Super Bowl and the Super Life

I used to negatively judge those people with metal detectors who troll the beach for lost treasures. I mentally criticized them for capitalizing on other people's misfortunes . . . that is, until I met Tommy.

One afternoon I was sitting on the beach in Maui when Tommy walked by, sweeping his metal detector. He looked happy and gave me a toothy grin.

I decided to venture beyond my opinions and make some contact with the fellow. "Ever find anything valuable?" I asked him.

"Sure!" he answered. "Some watches, lots of coins . . . and a Super Bowl ring."

"You found a Super Bowl ring?" I asked incredulously.

"Yep. A couple of years ago, I found a player's ring from the 1969 Super Bowl. That was the most famous one—when Joe Namath and the New York Jets overcame the 18-point odds against them to beat the Baltimore Colts, 16–7."

"What did you do with the ring?"

"I called the Jets' office and read someone the initials on the ring. Sure enough, there was a player with those initials who had come to Maui a year after the game and lost the ring in the ocean. It got buried in the sand until I detected it—29 years later."

"Did you sell him back the ring?"

"Of course not! Why would I want to charge him for the ring he lost? It belonged to him, and I was happy to return it. But then some reporters got wind of what had happened, so the player and his wife flew back here, and the media took all kinds of pictures and videos. I was famous for about five minutes."

Tommy laughed and added, "The player asked me if I wanted a reward; he said he'd give me whatever I wanted. I told him that I felt very blessed to simply be able to walk the beach every day at sunset and feel the beauty of nature around me. I have all the reward I need.

"Then the player's wife told me that she had friends in the airline business. She offered me free tickets whenever I wanted them. That was an offer I couldn't refuse. So now, every year my wife and I take a trip somewhere—usually first class. It's a great life, I must say."

When you live in harmony with your own values, life finds ingenious ways to take care of you. Take Tommy, for instance. He had no intention of becoming famous or capitalizing on the treasure he found; he merely did what he loved, and the universe supported him.

When most people seek fame or fortune, they have their values inverted . . . along with their perceived road to achievement. They believe that if they can become rich and famous, they'll be happy. In truth, it's the other way around: If you do what makes you happy, prosperity and acknowledgment will naturally follow.

This wonderful story also reminds us to be wary of falling prey to judgments and prejudices. We never know why others are doing what they're doing; it's highly likely that they're doing something with a reason or motivation entirely different from what we would expect. Assumptions are often limiting and self-defeating. But when you're willing to challenge your assumptions and reach out beyond judgments, you'll often find that the person you've judged is innocent, or you may even be able to identify with them.

The road to success begins right where you're standing. Instead of trying to figure out how you can fly away, discover how you can fly right where you are.

Take What You Have and Make What You Want

A fledgling Jewish congregation needed a building in which to hold their services. After searching for a long time, they found that the only space available in their town was a Christian church, so they signed a contract to rent the church's sanctuary for their Sabbath services.

On the first Saturday that services were held, a congregant came to the rabbi aghast and exclaimed, "There's a big cross on that wall!"

"Shhhhh . . ." the rabbi answered. "It's a 'T'—for 'Torah.'"

There are two ways that you can change your world: The first is to manipulate your environment—get rid of everything you don't like and import everything you do. This method works temporarily, but since no one can control their entire environment all the time, it eventually leads to disappointment, stress, and conflict.

The second way is to shift your attitude or viewpoint. While you can't control your outer world, you can always control how you think about it. Ultimately, your inner world is the only one in which you maintain autonomy and have access to the greatest freedom and joy.

When you find yourself in a situation beyond your control, find some way to look at it that brings you peace and relief. When you learn to develop a positive perspective, you recognize that your true domain of mastery lies in your attitude. As an ancient sage once noted, "He who conquers cities is great, but he who conquers his thoughts is greater."

You can make anything out of anything. Why not make it what you want?

Imminent Success

A young father stood at his kitchen window watching Billy, his six-year-old son, amuse himself in the backyard with a baseball and bat. The boy kept tossing the ball in the air, swinging at it with the bat, and missing. After a long time, Billy didn't manage to get even one hit, and his dad grew dismayed. Finally, the father could stand it no longer, so he decided to go out and say something comforting to his son.

He put his hand on Billy's shoulder and soberly told him, "Well, son, I guess you're just not cut out to be a hitter."

"Hitter?" Billy returned quickly. "Who cares about hitting? *I'm gonna be the greatest* pitcher *there ever was!"*

Failure is an interpretation, not a fact. The illusion of defeat is caused only by tunnel vision. Nothing is any one way all the time. Even a stopped clock is right twice a day. Negativity is a perceptual choice that you can reverse at will. If you hold a loss up to a higher light, you can turn it into a win.

We triumph not in spite of our mistakes, but *because* of them. If you're tempted to think of yourself as a "loser," reframe your self-image to become a "learner." Clever minds take things that go wrong and capitalize on them. Many a great teacher and leader grew into their power by overcoming adversity. Their challenges knocked them off their course for a moment, but later they were able to recognize that the obstacles were actually a part of their course.

Greatness lives within you. If you honor your personal strengths, you'll have all the tools you need to achieve your goals. If something you're doing isn't working, that's probably because it's disconnected from what you'd love to do. Tell the truth about what makes your heart sing, and you'll have your road map for success.

Trust Your Instincts

Ellen Ottenburg checked into a hospital in West Hills, California, to give birth to a baby girl. While mother and child were recuperating, the family's three Doberman pinschers mysteriously disappeared from their home. Ellen's husband was frantic, and he drove around the city for hours looking for the dogs, with no luck.

Late that night, Ellen looked out the window of her third-floor hospital room. What she saw amazed her: Sitting on the sidewalk were all three dogs, looking patiently up at her window and no worse for wear after traveling miles across busy city streets and highways.

Not only had the dogs managed to find the hospital, they knew which room she was in. And once the "three musketeers" saw Ellen in the window and realized that she was fine, they willingly went home with her husband.

— from *Bonkers!* magazine

Nature has infused all of its creatures with impeccable wisdom. When you're connected to your innate intelligence, you know how to get where you want to go. God's mind is in direct communication with yours; in fact, your mind *is* God's mind.

We call animals "dumb," but in many ways, they're smarter than humans—not because they have more intelligence, but because they access it more freely. Their instinctual knowing hasn't been overridden with social programming that distracts them from their nature. Animals accept themselves and their purpose as they are, and in such innocence, they're precisely guided.

All of nature knows its right place and finds it. You, too, have a right place. To access it, simply quiet your mind, listen to your inner voice, and let joy rather than fear be your guide. As you get into your own flow, you'll easily and naturally be connected with the perfect people and situations that match your mission and destiny.

You're not bereft, alone, or stupid. The brilliance of the entire universe is yours. You're truly a genius. Act on your inner knowing, and you'll find everything you could ever want or need.

Deliver Your Gift

A poet fell ill and complained to his doctor, "I have a rash and my joints ache. I get headaches and I can't sleep at night. I feel irritable and depressed."

The doctor thought for a moment and asked, "When was the last time you recited your poetry?"

"Several months ago," the poet answered.

"Have you read any of your latest poems aloud?"

"Not really."

"Then go ahead and share your favorite new poem with me," the doctor requested.

"All right," the poet said. Then he stood up and gave a compelling soliloquy.

"Excellent!" the doctor congratulated him. "May I please hear another?"

The poet recited another work.

"Keep going," the doctor encouraged.

After the poet had delivered several more of his poems, the doctor asked, "How do you feel now?"

Startled, the poet realized that he felt much better. "I feel wonderful!" he announced.

"Then go home and continue this," the doctor prescribed. "When you shut down your spirit, you shut down your body. If you keep expressing yourself, you'll be fine."

Health is a function of self-expression. When you live true to yourself and your dreams, your body, mind, and emotions will all line up with your intentions. When you don't express your truth, however, you'll become clogged, frustrated, and despondent.

Depression is a sign that you're denying your self-expression. You simply can't be expressing yourself and feel dispirited at the same time. If you should feel depressed, give voice to the energy moving inside you. Speak your truth and act on your creative impulses; the fog will quickly dissipate and you'll find yourself back on track with your purpose. Many people have even had illnesses disappear (including those considered incurable) when they reclaimed their right and power to live fully, freely, and from the heart.

You have a gift that *only you* can deliver. Do it. Suddenly everything else will seem less important, you'll feel strong and alive, and providence will move on your behalf.

The Best News

Roberto De Vincenzo, the renowned Argentinian golfer, once won a pro tournament with a substantial cash prize. After receiving the check and smiling for the cameras, he went to the clubhouse and prepared to leave.

Sometime later, he walked to his car in the parking lot and was approached by a young woman. She congratulated him on his victory and then told him that her baby was seriously ill and near death—she didn't know how she would ever pay the doctors' bills and hospital expenses.

De Vincenzo was touched by her story, and he took out a pen and endorsed his winning check over to the woman. "Make some good days for the child," he said as he pressed the check into her hand.

The next week, De Vincenzo was having lunch in a country club when a Professional Golf Association official came to his table. "Some of the boys in the parking lot told me you met a young woman there after you won that tournament last week."

De Vincenzo nodded.

"Well," said the official, "I have news for you—she's a phony. She has no sick kid. That girl fleeced you, my friend."

"You mean there's no dying baby?"

"That's right."

"That's the best news I've heard all week," De Vincenzo answered.

— from *The Best of Bits and Pieces*

Your happiness depends not on events, but on what you make of them. You can't control what other people do, but you do have total control over your own response. When you react out of fear or judgment, you compound the illusions that bring you pain. When your responses stem from a sense of love and trust, you dispel dark beliefs and open the door to grace.

Once you perform an act, release it to the universe. If your intentions are pure, then you're not responsible for what others make of what you do. Trust life to settle everything into its right place. If people distort or misuse what you've created, then they'll have to deal with the consequences . . . and that isn't your business. Your business is to live with a whole heart, act in harmony with your values, and find peace through your own integrity.

The meaning of any experience is what you give it. If others tempt you to step into fear or judgment, don't succumb—instead, choose the high road. The path to a peaceful heart is paved with peaceful interpretations. If you focus on evil, you'll only find more of it. If, however, you turn your attention to miracles, you'll discover them where you look. The world you see through the eyes of love is far closer to reality than the one shown to you by fear. Giving others the benefit of the doubt will bring relief to you both.

Be Your Own Beloved

At a seminar, a woman named Georgia reported that she'd been married to a man who was emotionally absent. After many long and frustrating years attempting to put the spark back into her marriage, Georgia felt she needed to leave her husband.

"I told him I wanted a divorce, but he refused to give it to me," she told the group. "So I decided that even if he *didn't love me,* I *would love me. I decided to give myself the love and tenderness I'd been seeking from him. So every day I wrote myself a long love letter telling myself how beautiful, wise, and desirable I am.*

"One day, my husband found one of the letters. Since it was unsigned, he assumed it was from another man. The next day he came to me, waving the letter in his hand. He said, 'I can't compete with this—you can have your divorce!'"

Your relationships are your mirrors: The love you receive—or don't receive—from others is a reflection of how much you're loving yourself. When you truly love yourself, you can never be abused. But when you don't love yourself, nobody on the planet will be able to save you.

If you feel sad or frustrated that you're not getting the love, appreciation, and acknowledgment that you crave from someone else, give it to yourself. It's your own love you want, so why confuse yourself by seeking it from another? When you honor and nurture yourself, your happiness will proceed from within you, and you won't have to depend on another for it.

As you give yourself more love, your relationships will change to reflect your self-honoring. You won't need to force or manipulate anyone; life will assist you in accomplishing the changes you desire. Those who don't match your self-appreciation will either begin to do so, or they'll leave your world of influence. And in turn, the universe will send you people who match your inner romance.

Another person isn't the source of your love—you are. True love is an inside job.

A Perfect Fit

A man went to Zumbach the tailor to be fitted for a new suit. After Zumbach altered the suit, the man stood in front of the mirror to examine the fit. He noticed that the jacket's right sleeve was rather short.

"Say, Zumbach," he noted, "this sleeve looks a little short. Would you please lengthen it?"

"The sleeve isn't too short," the tailor answered emphatically. "Your arm is too long. Just pull it back a few inches, and you'll see that the sleeve fits perfectly."

The man lifted his arm a bit, and indeed the sleeve was matched with his wrist. But this motion affected the upper portion of the jacket. "Now the nape of the collar is several inches above my neck," he complained.

"There's nothing wrong with the collar," Zumbach responded. "Your neck is too low. Lift the back of your neck and it will fit just right."

The man raised his back and neck a bit—sure enough, the collar rounded it where it was supposed to. But now there was another problem: The bottom of the jacket was resting high above the man's seat.

"Now my whole rear end is sticking out!" the customer exclaimed.

"No problem," Zumbach returned. "Just lift it up so that it stays under the jacket."

Again the man complied, which left his body in a very contorted posture. Zumbach had convinced him that the problem wasn't with the suit, but with him. So the customer paid the tailor for the suit and walked out on to the street in a most awkward position, struggling to keep all the parts of the suit in their right places.

Soon two women passed him as he walked along, and they bid him a good morning. A few moments later, one woman turned to the other and commented, "That poor man is really crippled!"

"He sure is," the other replied. "But his suit fits great!"

Our families, friends, schools, religions, and societies impose many suits upon us. Some of them fit, but many of them don't. If a job, relationship, living situation, or spiritual path doesn't sit well with you, others may try to convince you that *you're* the problem. A good, wise, talented, or mature person, they'll say, should be able to step into this position, handle it well, and even enjoy it. But if it doesn't correspond to your soul and intentions, you only cripple yourself by trying to stuff yourself into a position that doesn't fit you at all.

What truly matches you will feel right and enhance who you already are. It will allow you room to breathe and express yourself naturally. The more you have to alter yourself or live a lie to keep a situation going, the more you can be certain it isn't for you. The true test of a relationship, job, or religion is that you can fully and freely be yourself in it. Anything that's good for you will bring out your best and won't force you to make believe that you're something you're not.

A GIFT AWAITS

The big day was finally here. Denny had set a goal to run the famous Pikes Peak Marathon for his 50th birthday, and now he stood at the starting line. For a year he had arduously trained to master the grueling race, which was 13 miles up the steep Colorado mountain, and 13 miles back down.

Denny surprised himself with the speed and strength of his ascent, but he began to feel tired as he made his way down. Then he got stuck behind a slow runner, and the narrow path through the woods forced Denny to hang back and wait for an opening to pass. For a long time he had to lag behind the fellow in front of him, who was struggling to maintain even a moderate pace. Denny grumbled to himself that no one so out of shape should be allowed to run a marathon. Meanwhile, the back of the man's T-shirt kept staring Denny in the face: **Bob's #4.** *Denny grew curious about the meaning of those words.*

Finally Denny found an opportunity to pass. As he overtook the runner, who was huffing and puffing, Denny asked him, "What's 'Bob's #4?'"

"My friend Bob had a dream to run this marathon four times in his life," answered the fellow between breaths. "He ran it three times, but then last year he died. So I decided to complete his dream for him. This is Bob's #4."

Suddenly, Denny, who had felt exhausted, found new inspiration to finish the race.

We may be tempted to judge people or events that seem to be standing in our way, yet what appears to be a roadblock may offer us an important lesson or blessing. We never know for sure why anyone does anything. Other people have their own reasons for their actions, and often there's a meaning that we don't recognize at first glance.

If you can resist the temptation to judge or lash out with a knee-jerk response, then you'll find this valuable insight: *Everything happens for a purpose, and everything serves*. The entire world is our classroom, and every person is our teacher.

Usually when others seem to be against us, that isn't even their intention. They may simply be upset about something unrelated to us, or in fear or pain for a reason we don't understand—so don't take their actions personally. If they seem evil, they're simply wounded. Do your best to be kind anyway and keep your thoughts above victimization or conflict. Compassion for others is a gift we give ourselves. When the time is right, the situation will be resolved and you'll be glad that you held the greater perspective.

If things seem to be moving too slowly or not falling into place as you had planned, it won't do you any good to push harder. Pushing harder only makes things go slower. Perhaps there's something else you're meant to be doing for the moment. If you turn your attention from the obstacle and do something else that comes more easily and joyfully, you'll understand why you were impeded. Then the roadblock will clear, and you'll be able to handle your task easily and deftly.

29

Take the Best and Leave the Rest

A great sage was known all across the land for his profound wisdom and brilliant guidance. Many people traveled far and wide to sit at his feet and absorb his vast knowledge.

One day he told his students, "I have a confession to make. A wizard has placed a spell on me. This spell brings with it news both good and bad. The good news is that half of what I tell you is the absolute truth, direct from the mouth of God. If you grasp this wisdom and put it into practice, your life will change in miraculous ways and you'll experience lifelong happiness.

"The bad news is that the other half of what I tell you is pure illusion and a horrible distortion of truth. If you follow this guidance, your life will be ruined and you'll be sorry you ever met me.

"My dilemma, my friends, is that I don't know which is which."

Every great spiritual teaching was initiated by a prophet who had a unique insight into truth. Over time, however, people with more limited, fearful, and self-protective interests added their own elements, which weren't in harmony with the teachings and intentions of the founder. After many years of interpretation and word of mouth (much like the game "Telephone"), a system of belief developed that resulted in a mix of many different views, some pure and others distorted.

Some teachers tell you that you're not smart enough to know what's true, so you must rely on the guidance of those wiser than you. Of course other people can help at times; but at the same time, you *are* very wise indeed—and you're too smart to make believe that you don't know. Ultimately you must trust your inner guidance. When you hear an idea that's right and true for you, it rings in your heart like a familiar bell. Information that doesn't match your purpose falls flat and makes no sense. The wise student takes the best and leaves the rest. Eventually the truth will make itself known.

Your relationship with your Higher Power is as unique as your fingerprints or personality. Have faith in a teacher or religion, but temper it with discernment. *Honor your own knowing.*

Feed Your Heart

The ancient Chinese language is comprised of symbols for words, called "characters." Each character represents an idea and combinations of characters form words. In that language, the character for "busy" is a combination of two others— the characters for "killing" and "heart."

Busyness is largely self-distraction. We fear facing our feelings and ourselves, so we generate an endless list of errands, tasks, and appointments to keep us occupied. Then we get frazzled, stressed, and uptight, which put intimacy and play on the back burner until they're completely out of sight.

It's no surprise that heart disease is so prevalent in our culture. Our hearts need time and space to flow with a sane rhythm of life. But even more than our physical hearts, we need to nurture our emotional hearts. If we give love to ourselves and others, our hearts will be happy and healthy, both physically *and* emotionally.

Take the time you need to enjoy your life. You can allow yourself pleasure and still fulfill your responsibilities. And if you keep your spirit happy, you'll actually accomplish your tasks more quickly, easily, and efficiently. Each day, set aside time to nourish your soul. Explore music, art, or dance; read for pleasure; get together with friends; play with your pet; engage in a hobby; or get out in nature. When you do something you love for even a short time each day, you'll recharge your batteries and find the strength and energy to do the things you need to do.

If you're too busy to connect with your spirit, you're just too busy. Honor your spirit as you go, and all else will follow naturally.

31

TRUE COMPASSION

Twice in my life I have experienced deep depression. Both times various friends tried to rescue me with well-intended encouragement and advice. . . .

In the midst of my depression, I had a friend who took a different tack. Every afternoon at around four o'clock he came to me, sat me in a chair, removed my shoes, and massaged my feet. He hardly said a word, but he was there, he was with me. He was a lifeline for me, a link to the human community and thus to my own humanity. He had no need to "fix" me. He knew the meaning of compassion.

— Parker J. Palmer

When you observe a loved one in a painful situation, your discomfort may tempt you to jump in and rescue them. While your intensions are good, they don't need to be rescued; what they need is kindness, support, and permission to just be who they are. Often our notion of how others *should* proceed is an imposition of our beliefs and values over theirs, which only compounds their pain.

To heal is to bring relief—not as we think others should be relieved, but in a way that will actually help them. Being compassionate is discovering what makes someone else happy, and then delivering it to them.

The first step to helping a loved one out of trouble is to just be with them. Let them know you love and care about them. Your presence is more important than your technique—words are the least important element of healing. Take refuge in the silent sanctuary of now. To simply be with another person as they move through their process is a high and holy gift. If you resist their challenge or their response to it, you'll just aggravate their difficulty. If you show them unconditional love, you'll help them more than any quick-fix remedy ever could.

An Abundant Universe

The Tlingit tribe of Native Americans (who have long resided in Alaska) once lived in a rich and prosperous world. During salmon season, it was said that the streams were so full of fish that a person could cross a stream simply by stepping across the salmon! The Tlingits lived in such a consciousness of abundance that they had no word in their language for "starve."

Picture the world that the Tlingits inhabited, and behold the universe as God created it: abundant, with enough of everything for everyone. All sense of lack exists only in our minds. Insufficiency isn't a fact; it's a state of consciousness. When you think "lack," everything you see is deficient. But this works for prosperity, too. When you see through the eyes of "enoughness," you'll find that there's plenty everywhere. Not only is life capable of supplying enough food for everyone, it can also provide enough love, well-being, safety, success, and joy.

Your experience of prosperity depends on the thoughts you dwell upon. Take care not to go into mass agreement of lack or loss. It's easy to get swept up in talk of an ailing economy, terrorism, or "the flu going around." Yet no matter what others are saying or doing, you have the power to choose the world you live in by right of your consciousness. You're a sovereign entity generating your own experience. You can create or dismantle any belief at any time.

All thoughts of prosperity are in harmony with your true nature and purpose, and the universe as God created it. Practice thinking rich, and you'll realize just how rich you are.

Reach into Majesty

Gamble everything for love, if you're a true human being. If not, leave this gathering.

Half-heartedness doesn't reach into majesty. You set out to find God, but then you keep stopping for long periods at mean-spirited roadhouses.

— Rumi

The key to success is to stay true to your intentions. Your life is a perfect mirror of your intentions—life gives you exactly what you give it. If you enter into a relationship, career, or life path with a whole heart, you'll enjoy a whole result. But if you invest only half a heart, you'll get half a result.

You can't stand over a gap with your feet straddling both sides. Jump one way or the other, but whatever you do, *jump all the way*. Either way, you'll gain. You'll only lose if you waver in the middle. Look before you leap—then leap.

Along the spiritual path, many distractions beckon. Fear, mistrust, and illusion await you at many turns and beguile you to shut down your heart and protect yourself from evil forces. If you happen to fall prey to these tempters, just pick yourself up and move on. You'll be stronger for the experience and less likely to buy faulty goods the next time.

Everything that shows up before you is an element in your quest. Use each experience to practice finding truth, and you'll transform mean-spirited roadhouses into way stations to enlightenment.

Allow Life

Sitting quietly,
doing nothing,
spring comes,
and the grass
grows by itself.

— Zen saying

Sometimes we forget that we're human *beings*, and we act like human *doings*. We believe that if we didn't anxiously manipulate life, everything would crumble around us. Yet the universe is doing quite well on its own: Well-being abounds, and good things happen to us—not because of our attempts to protect ourselves, but in spite of them.

Allow life to unfold naturally. A profound intelligence is guiding the universe, far beyond your conscious control. At this moment, your own body is performing billions of complex processes to keep you living. You don't have to tell your lungs to breathe, your heart to beat, or your stomach to digest your food. Something inside you knows how to perform these functions, and does so effortlessly and efficiently. That "something" is everywhere, and it's brilliantly orchestrating the universe.

Don't do something for the sake of doing something—act only when you're guided from within. If you don't know what to *do,* just *be*. Let nature take its course, through and around you.

What You're Worth

Self-loving

is not so

vile a sin as

self-neglecting.

— William
Shakespeare

It isn't selfish to love yourself—it's the first step to true kindness. Only when you love who and what you are can you love others in the way that they yearn to be cared for.

Very few people err by loving themselves too much; most err by loving themselves too little. Guilt and self-punishment are far more destructive than self-indulgence. The greatest gift you can give yourself is permission to be yourself and express what's inside you.

If you imagine that your inner promptings are proceeding from wisdom and you act upon them, you'll go much further than if you doubt or deny them. Don't talk yourself out of greatness. Many have, and the world has lost out because of it. Great strides are accomplished by those who are presumptuous enough to believe that they might have a contribution to make.

When you recognize what you're worth, you'll take care of yourself as you deserve. Then you'll be in a golden position to help others.

RESIGNATION FROM ADULTHOOD

I've decided that I'd like to accept the responsibilities of an eight-year-old again.

I want to go to McDonald's and think that it's a four-star restaurant. I want to sail sticks across a fresh mud puddle and make ripples in a pond with rocks. I want to think M & M's are better than money because you can eat them. I want to lie under a big oak tree and run a lemonade stand with my friends on a hot summer day.

I want to think the world is fair, that people are honest and good. I want to believe that anything is possible. I want to be oblivious to the complexities of life and be overly excited by the little things. I want to live simply again. I don't want my days to consist of computer crashes, paperwork, depressing news, more days in the month than money in the bank, doctor bills, gossip, illness, and the loss of loved ones.

I want to believe in the power of smiles, hugs, kind words, truth, justice, peace, dreams, imagination, humankind, and making angels in the snow.

So . . . here's my checkbook, my car keys, my credit card bill, and my 401(k) statements. I'm officially resigning from adulthood. And if you want to discuss this further, you'll have to catch me first, 'cause . . . tag—you're It!

P.S. I love you.

The fall from Grace we read about in the Bible didn't occur millions of years ago in the Garden of Eden—it occurred in your life shortly after you were born. In truth, you can never fall from Grace, but you can forget that you're constantly surrounded by it. As the mystic poet Kabir noted, "I laugh when I hear that the fish in water is thirsty."

Children are magnificent teachers because they live in innocence. All of us are born in *simplicity,* but then we learn *complexity*. By watching children, we can reclaim the innocence we gave away. Kids live in the moment, play frequently, let their imaginations soar, ask for what they want, let their emotions rise and fall, laugh often, have no sense of shame, don't believe that they have to earn their good, and don't fear death. They're in touch with their natural knowing and live fully from it.

It's never too late to have a happy childhood. To do so, simply drop what you've been taught and remember what you know. Experience moves us away from innocence, but then returns us to it. If you play as you go, your health problems will disappear, your career will yield abundance, and your relationships will be exhilarating.

Simple delight beckons. Will you come home to it?

Natural Healing

The witch doctor succeeds for the same reason all the rest of us succeed. Each patient carries his own doctor inside himself. . . . We are at our best when we give the doctor who resides within each patient a chance to go to work.

— Albert Schweitzer

Who is the physician?
Only the mind of the patient himself.

— from *A Course in Miracles*

The art of medicine consists of amusing the patient while nature cures the disease.

— Voltaire

The true healer lives inside of you. While outside agents such as doctors and medicine may seem to be effecting a cure (or not), they only play out your intentions. No doctor or medicine can help a patient who's made a choice for illness, and no doctor or medicine is necessary for one who's made a choice for wellness.

Life is always seeking balance: If you pave over a meadow, tiny blades of grass will find their way through the cracks within a short time. Eventually the new shoots will displace the pavement altogether and the meadow will be restored. Nature always bats last.

To return to your natural state of health, let yourself be. Don't crimp your lifeline with fear, resistance, or fighting what is. Do things for yourself that make you happy. Align your words, thoughts, and actions with your goals, and don't be distracted by obstacles. Magnify and celebrate everything that matches your intention, and stay light. Know that you're worthy of healing and that God wants happiness for you as much as you want it for yourself—or even more.

As you claim well-being as your birthright, you'll enjoy radiant aliveness, boundless energy, and exhilarating freedom. The universe is conspiring to maintain your wellness, and it calls upon you to join it.

Searching and Finding

Those that go searching
for love only make
manifest their own
lovelessness, and the
loveless never find
love, only the loving
find love, and
they never
have to seek it.

— D. H. Lawrence

Searching for love is the great quest of life, for love is our true nature—and nothing less will satisfy us. Yet where we search for love makes all the difference in whether or not we find it.

All the love you seek is within you. When you look for love from the outside world, you might receive momentary spikes of happiness, but ultimately you'll be left feeling empty, frustrated, and confused. No one can give you what you already have. Return to your inner fountain of happiness, and you'll be eternally replenished. There you'll find so much fulfillment that you'll be overflowing with it and will have plenty to share with others.

The secret of life isn't to *get* love, it's to *give* it. The love you give to others flows through you and lifts you as you radiate it. When you take your attention off your own difficulties and find the beauty in others and the world, you'll remember your own. In truth, you were never lacking—you just needed a reminder that you already had love.

At this moment, you're enfolded in infinite love, for the arms of God hold and caress you. Recognize your eternal lovability, and you'll become a lover unlike any the world has ever known.

Your Treasured World

If a man is called to be a street sweeper, he should sweep streets even as Michelangelo painted, or Beethoven played music, or Shakespeare wrote poetry. He should sweep streets so well that all the hosts of heaven and earth will pause to say, "Here lived a great street sweeper, who did his job well."

— Dr. Martin Luther King, Jr.

No task is too small a vehicle for greatness. We've been taught to equate success with amassing fame and fortune, but true achievement is born in the way we execute life's details. To master the big picture of life, begin with what is before you *now.*

Immerse your heart and mind in whatever you're doing. Be fully present with the task at hand and you'll lift it, along with yourself, into majesty. You're not responsible for changing the entire world—you're responsible for uplifting the world you touch. Make your world a treasured place, and you'll bring joy and healing to everyone who comes into it. Then *they'll* be inspired to pass it along to an ever-widening sphere of influence.

Foolish minds are lured by the flamboyant at the expense of substance. Success isn't measured by where you end up, but by how you journey. Take pride in everything you do so that when you go to sleep at night, you'll rest with a happy heart, for you'll know that you gave all you could. God could never ask for more.

Your life is your kingdom—rule it with pride and grace. Your creations will praise your endowment, and you'll reap all the riches a soul could seek.

Light and Free

After his famous sojourn at Walden Pond, Henry David Thoreau went to visit his friend and fellow literary luminary, Ralph Waldo Emerson. Thoreau offered Emerson a detailed account of the wisdom and inspiration he'd gained from his time living in the woods by himself.

Emerson listened intently to Thoreau's account and then asked, "What would you say is the most important lesson you learned at Walden?"

Thoreau answered authoritatively, "Simplify, simplify, simplify."

Emerson thought for a moment and then responded, "I think one 'simplify' would have done quite well."

Spiritual growth doesn't require us to *add* to ourselves, it invites us to *let go* of everything that encumbers us. The world has taught us that success is a matter of acquiring and having, yet we find that the more stuff we collect, the less we know ourselves, and the further we drift from peace.

Owning things is fun . . . until they own us. We need to rethink what we have and why. For instance, our sophisticated technology gives us devices to save time, but then we fill our newfound free time with more stuff to do, so we end up becoming busier and more stressed, not more relaxed. We say yes to countless requests—fully intending to carry them out—only to discover that most projects require more time and energy than we anticipated. Then we feel overwhelmed with all that's on our plate, so we grow irritable and wonder how we got burnt out.

At some point, we recognize that less is more. When we quit trying to prove or protect ourselves with possessions, accolades, or degrees, we begin to see beauty and worth in ourselves, *as we are*. Then we find immense joy in lightening up—for the lighter we get, the higher we can soar. We gain freedom in releasing possessions, activities, and relationships that stifle our happiness, and begin to appreciate the simple things in life. The white space on a page is as important as the ink. The silence between the words is as compelling as the words themselves. Rest is as important as activity. As we recognize that simplicity is the flower that brings the intellect to its knees, we own the greatest riches of all.

TRUE TO YOURSELF

Gray mentions a case in a patient who would go out of a door, close it, and then come back, uncertain as to whether he had closed it, close it again, go off a little way, again feel uncertain as to whether he closed it properly, go back again, and so on for many times. Hammond relates the history of a case in an intelligent man who in undressing for bed would spend an hour or two determining whether he should first take off his coat or his shoes. In the morning he would sit for an hour with his stockings in his hand, unable to determine which he should put on first. . . .

— from *Anomalies and Curiosities of Medicine* (1896)
by George M. Gould and Walter L. Pyle

For God's sake, choose a self and stand by it!

— William James

Personal power isn't so much a matter of what you decide, but that you *do* decide. What makes many leaders great is their ability to stand behind their choices. Honor your choices because they're your own.

Often there's no single right or wrong way to approach a situation—any path you adhere to with intention and integrity will take you where you want to go. As the Chinese oracle *I Ching* reminds us, "Perseverance furthers." When you choose a path and stay with it, your true self will begin to shine, and your life will change in amazing ways. You'll feel free and whole, and you'll attract friends who will support you in your choice. Some people may leave your life, but others who better match you will take their place. Most important, you'll be at peace with yourself as you realize that all God ever wanted you to be is what you are.

You must make a stand for who you are. This is a challenge for most people, since who you actually are may be quite different from who the world asks you to be. You've adopted many masks in your life in response to what others expect from you. Yet behind all of your facades, there's a self who feels real and empowered when you become it. This self isn't to be minimized or denied; it's to be celebrated. If you can live as your true self, rather than as the cardboard person the world would make of you, you'll find the strength and courage to activate and enjoy your true choices.

Bring a Large Cup

A busy woman grew overwhelmed and frustrated with her life, so she went to visit her guru for advice.

He listened to her story and said, "The answer is obvious: Get rid of the bad and keep only the good."

The woman went home and evaluated what was working in her life and what wasn't. She methodically released what didn't bring her joy and kept only what energized her. Her life changed for the better, and her heart found greater peace.

A year later, she again felt burdened and confused. Again she sojourned to her guru and told him of her predicament.

"I have your answer," the master responded. "Let go of the good and keep only the great."

The woman returned to the world she'd built and once again sorted out her life, this time releasing what was merely good but not great. She decided that from that moment on, she'd live just from joy and only participate in those activities that she found empowering.

Another year went by, and again she felt stuck. Once more she flew to her teacher and reported her distress.

"I will tell you what to do," the sage replied. "Go home and really practice now: Let go of the great and keep only the magnificent."

Don't settle for a merely good or even great life. Make magnificence your benchmark. Keep opening to greater vistas. Wholeheartedly love and master what's before you so that it will lead you to your next greater step. Release what isn't working in your life and reach higher. Life isn't about adapting, surviving, and putting out fires—it's about expanding, deepening, and surfing on the cutting edge of your aliveness.

The day will never come when you wake up and say, "There, everything's done!" You may arrive at plateaus where you enjoy resting and savoring for a while, but the time will come when you'll be ready to move on and do more. For every achievement you accomplish, there's one beyond it that will lead you to even greater fulfillment.

Your journey will go from good to better to best if you realize that every choice you make offers you an opportunity to live your truth more impeccably. From time to time, survey your possessions, living space, job, friendships, and recreational activities. Ask of each aspect, "Does this match my joy and bring me life?" If so, carry on in high style; if not, either let it go or upgrade it so that it honors your true intention.

Movement is a sign of life. Sometimes there is greater spiritual security in launching into uncharted territory than in lingering in a familiar but stagnant situation. Trust that if you're following your deepest guidance, your move will serve others—for as you reach for your highest good, you'll support them to claim theirs. Love never says goodbye; it only expands to embrace greater hellos.

Life will fill any cup you bring it . . . so bring it a large one.

You Already Know

Whenever you're called
on to make up your mind.
And you're hampered by
not having any,
The best way to solve the
dilemma, you'll find
Is simply by spinning a penny.
No, not so that chance shall
decide the affair
While you're passively standing
there moping,
But the moment the penny
is up in the air
You suddenly know
what you're hoping.

— "A Psychological Tip," by Piet Hein

If you have difficulty making a decision, examine how you feel about each of the choices. There's a place inside you that already knows what you want, and when you're honest about how you feel, the decision will be resolved effortlessly.

When you find yourself unable to decide between two options, take a coin and assign one alternative to heads, and the other to tails. Flip the coin and imagine that the side that comes up will be the path you're absolutely going to follow. The moment you see which side appears, notice your immediate gut reaction. Do you feel happy or disappointed? Energized or deflated? Enlivened or depressed? Recognize how you feel, and you'll see that your inner guidance is speaking to you through your sense of joy or its absence.

If thinking about something doesn't feel right, then doing it will probably feel worse. You can think things through up until a point, but then you must consult your heart before finally acting. Decision making is a lot simpler than you've been taught.

How would you like this situation to turn out? Spend more time thinking about the outcome you desire and less on the one you fear, and you'll see that the path to happiness is paved with joy—follow it now, and you'll end up where you want to be.

Common Ground

Rabbi Goldstein and Father Quinn were seated next to each other at an ecumenical dinner. The dishes were cleared, coffee was served, and the two men were discussing their vocations.

"Tell me, Father," inquired the rabbi, "is there room for advancement in your profession?"

"Well, yes," answered Father Quinn. "The next level above mine is bishop. There's one bishop in this city—it's possible that one day I could serve in that capacity."

"Very nice," the rabbi commented. "How about beyond that?"

"Beyond bishop is cardinal. Now, mind you, I'm not an ambitious man, but if God willed it, I could step into that role."

"That's nice," answered Rabbi Goldstein. "And beyond that?"

"The highest rank in our church is, of course, the Pope. Believe me, Rabbi, I don't sit around and think about being the Pope. But when the

Pope is called to Heaven, the cardinals get together and pray. Then God whispers divine inspiration to them and they name a new Pope. If, by some stretch of the imagination, I was chosen, I would pray to fulfill the position with humility and love."

"Of course," the rabbi responded. "What then, Father? Could you go higher than Pope?"

By this time, Father Quinn had grown perturbed with the rabbi's questioning. Irritated, he threw down his napkin and spouted, "Good God, man! Who do you expect me to become—Jesus Christ?"

"Why not?" Rabbi Goldstein answered with a sneaky smile. "One of our boys made it!"

While every religion has unique rituals and dogma, all seek to connect us with our spiritual source. They all honor the reality and presence of God; the importance of love, compassion, and kindness; and the eternalness of life. These basic truths far outshine the individual ways religions express them. We can honor our differences while celebrating our unity—then we can meet on common ground.

Some people have used religion as an excuse to put others down, or to draw lines in the sand, or to compete and kill. Some claim God is on their side and pray for help to win wars over infidels. Nothing could be further from God's will.

God is on everyone's side, and on no side at all. God is the Life Force that animates all living creatures, and loves all equally. God isn't a personality that fights or competes—God is Pure Energy, directed however we choose with our free will. We can use our power to heal or to destroy.

Those who argue over God overlook the presence of God. Lovers of God are lovers of God's children—*all* of us—and they seek to find meeting points, not dissension. Debating over whose God is more real, or competing and one-upping one another only distracts us from the fulfillment we yearn for. All paths eventually lead to the same mountaintop.

45

Look Inside

Stop this day and night with
me and you shall possess
the origin of all poems,
You shall possess the good
of the earth and sun. . . .
You shall no longer take things
at second or third hand, nor
look through the eyes of the dead,
nor feed on the spectres in books,
You shall not look through my eyes
either, nor take things from me,
You shall listen to all sides and
filter them from your self. . . .
And I know that the hand of
God is the promise of my own. . . .

— from "Song of Myself,"
by Walt Whitman

When you photocopy an image over many generations, the picture becomes distorted to the point that it bears little relationship to the original and is unrecognizable. In the same way, you can't have a secondhand relationship with God—your true power lies in your *direct* connection with Spirit. If you try to know God through the interpretations of many who came before you, you won't know God—you'll end up knowing others' perceptions, which are often tainted with fear and guilt and are not at all an expression of love.

If you depend on others to define God for you or dictate your path to peace, you'll grow confused, and your relationship with your Source will be diluted. Put aside everything anyone else has ever told you about God, truth, and life (which are all the same thing), and develop your own understanding and connection. All that ever was is before you now, and it beckons unto you to know it in your own way.

Forget what you've been *taught*, so you can remember what you *know*.

Stay Awake

A man came to Buddha and asked him, "Are you the Messiah?"

"No," answered Buddha.

"Then are you a saint?"

"No."

"Then are you a teacher?" the student persisted.

"No."

"Then what are you?" asked the student, exasperated.

"I am awake," Buddha answered.

We tend to want to fit people into categories. But because we're spiritual beings, any category into which we could fit ourselves or others only makes us seem smaller than we are. Ultimately titles and classifications create more separation than unity and end up distancing us from each other.

Wise, loving, or spiritually attuned people are no different from the rest of us; they simply remember who they are. Any truly enlightened teacher will tell you that all the best that they are, you are, too.

Every time you put a famous, beautiful, or gifted person on a pedestal and worship them, you diminish yourself. Celebrate their talents, but not at the expense of your own—honor them along with your own. Regard luminaries not as idols to be worshiped, but as role models to emulate. Then, as you draw forth your own strengths, you'll stand not below them as a student, but beside them as a peer.

The goal of all spiritual practice is simply to awaken. There is no one to become, but there is someone to recognize. Remember your true self, and you'll become one with your mentor. Why become a Buddhist when you could become the Buddha?

Brothers After All

Every part of the earth is sacred to my people. Every shining pine needle, every sandy shore, every mist in the dark woods, every clearing and humming insect is holy in the memory and experience of my people. . . . We are part of the earth and it is part of us. The perfumed flowers are our sisters, the deer, the horse, the great eagle, these are our brothers. The rocky crests, the juices in the meadows, the body heat of the pony, and man—all belong to the same family . . . you must remember that [the land] *is sacred, and you must teach your children that it is sacred and that each ghostly reflection in the clear water of the lakes tells of events and memories in the life of my people . . . what is there to life if a man cannot hear the lonely cry of the whippoorwill or the arguments of the frogs around a pond at night? . . . The air is precious to the red man, for all things share the same breath. . . . The wind that gave our grandfather his first breath also receives his last sigh. . . . I have seen a thousand rotting buffaloes on the prairie, left by the white man who shot them from a passing train. . . . What is man without beasts? If all the beasts were gone, man would die from great loneliness of spirit. For whatever happens to beasts, soon happens to man. All things are connected. . . . Whatever befalls the earth befalls the sons of the earth. If men spit upon the ground, they spit upon themselves. This we know: the earth does not belong to man; man belongs to the earth. . . . All things are connected like the blood which unites one family. . . . Man did not weave the web of life, he is merely a strand in it. Whatever he does to the web he does to himself. . . . We may be brothers after all. . . . One thing which we know, which the white man may one day discover—our God is the same God.*

— attributed to Chief Seattle,
Native American, in 1854

Our relationship with the earth is as real as our connection with each other; in some ways it runs even deeper. Our planet is the source of all physical bounty and the provider of sustenance for all living things. It isn't a commodity to be exploited, but a living, breathing being pulsating in a vibrant energy field. Mother Earth is far more sensitive to how we treat her than many people imagine—and far more resilient.

You can learn all of life's lessons by observing nature. For many thousands of years, indigenous peoples have lived in harmony with the spirit of the land, respecting it, taking no more than they needed, and striving to replenish the land in return. As our culture has drifted away from our relationship with the natural world, we've become alienated from ourselves. To revitalize ourselves, we must approach our environment with deeper respect and reverence.

Pray for the earth as you would a beloved relative. Picture a light in your heart expanding to embrace the entire globe. Visualize healing energy penetrating our planet to its very core. Picture the world as it was in its natural original state—teeming with life and rich, green, lush vegetation. Hold in your mind the image of clean air and water, with people of many different cultures living in harmony with *all* life forms.

Our world will transform in response to our appreciation. We should celebrate the beauty of nature wherever we find it, for we're richly blessed to live here. Let's open our hearts to reclaim our rightful place in the great web of creation. As we love and respect our planet, we'll heal ourselves as well as our world.

What to Give for Happiness

Life has loveliness to sell,
All beautiful and splendid things,
Blue waves whitened on a cliff,
Soaring fire that sways and sings
And children's faces looking up
Holding wonder like a cup.

Life has loveliness to sell,
Music like a curve of gold,
Scent of pine trees in the rain,
Eyes that love you, arms that hold,
And for the spirit's still delight,
Holy thoughts that star the night.

Spend all you have for loveliness,
Buy it and never count the cost;
For one white singing hour of peace
Count many a year of strife well lost,
And for a breath of ecstasy
Give all you have been, or could be.

— "Barter," by Sarah Teasdale

What would you give for happiness? Your money? Your possessions? Your career? You can't buy happiness; after all, *things* don't hold the most value in your life—*relationships* do. And relationships aren't built on what you get, but what you give. The only way to get happiness is to give one thing: your whole heart.

What makes your heart sing? Deny your calling no longer: When you find a person, home, career, or life path that you love, give yourself fully to it. Giving love, faith, and commitment costs you nothing and gets you everything.

You *can* have it all. The universe is capable of answering your every prayer. To receive your blessings, you must be willing to invest in them. Your most powerful investment is *yourself.* If you're going to participate in something, be *total.* Do it all the way or not at all. Action is important, but spirit is crucial.

You have access to infinite resources, and many gifts are being laid at your doorstep. Bring your dreams to life by being true to them.

HIDDEN SPLENDOR

I am your friend and my love for you goes deep. There is nothing I can give you which you have not got; but there is much, very much, that, while I cannot give it, you can take.

No heaven can come to us unless our hearts find rest in today. Take heaven! No peace lies in the future which is not hidden in this present little instant. Take peace!

The gloom of the world is but a shadow. Behind it, yet within our reach, is joy. There is radiance and glory in the darkness, could we but see—and to see we have only to look. I beseech you to look.

Life is so generous a giver, but we, judging its gifts by the covering, cast them away as ugly or heavy or hard. Remove the covering and you will find beneath it a living splendor, woven of love, by wisdom, with power.

Welcome it, grasp it, and you touch the angel's hand that brings it to you. Everything we call a trial, a sorrow, or a duty, believe me, that angel's hand is there, the gift is there, and the wonder of an overshadowing presence. Our joys, too; be not content with them as joys. They too conceal diviner gifts.

Life is so full of meaning and purpose, so full of beauty—beneath its covering—that you will find earth but cloaks your heaven.

Courage, then, to claim it; that is all; but courage you have, and the knowledge that we are pilgrims together, wending through unknown country home.

And so, at this time, I greet you. Not quite as the world sends greetings, but with profound esteem and with the prayer that for you now and forever, the day breaks, and the shadows flee away.

— Brother Giovanni, 1513

This stirring letter, written by a monk nearly 500 years ago, is still compelling today. All the comfort you seek is offered within it, so consider it a love letter that a dear friend has written to you.

Whenever you feel trapped in fear or confusion, you're responding to appearances. Brother Giovanni reminds us to look deeper—find the message or gift behind the storyline, and the challenge will transform to become your friend.

The thought that a situation is a problem is an interpretation, not a fact. In Arabic, the word for *problem* is translated as "another view." When you're faced with a problem, you're being invited to find another perspective from which to regard it. As you reframe it in your favor, you'll discover that it hasn't come to hurt you, but to help you. As author Richard Bach noted: "There is no such thing as a problem without a gift for you in its hands." When you discover and appreciate the gift, the problem will disappear.

Every word, thought, or action you generate is affirming either your problem or your solution. Many people argue for their limitations as if they offered them security, but they only end up keeping themselves trapped in a small and painful world. Become an advocate for your possibilities, not your limits. Never speak disparagingly of yourself or an experience. Hold firm to the vision of your intentions, and you'll have them. And when you're tempted to name something a "problem," call it a "project," "invitation," or "opportunity" instead. Then you'll be on course for the solution.

You're doing better than you think you are. Great love surrounds, enfolds, and fills you. You do not walk alone. Step forward with your head held high, and life will affirm all that you were born to be and do.

The Touch of the Master's Hand

'Twas battered and scarred, and the auctioneer
Thought it scarcely worth his while
To waste his time on the old violin,
But he held it up with a smile:
"What am I bidden, good folks?" he cried,
"Who'll start the bidding for me?"
"A dollar, a dollar"; then, "Two!" "Only two?
Two dollars, and who'll make it three?
Three dollars, once; three dollars, twice;
Going for three . . ." But no,
From the room, far back, a gray-bearded man
Came forward and picked up the bow;
Then, wiping the dust from the old violin,
And tightening up the strings,
He played a melody pure and sweet as a caroling angel sings.

The music ceased, and the auctioneer, with a voice that was quiet and low,

Said, "What am I bid for the old violin?" and he held it up with the bow.

"A thousand dollars, and who'll make it two?

Two thousand! And who'll make it three?

Three thousand, once; three thousand, twice,

And going, and gone," said he.

The people cheered, but some of them cried,

"We do not quite understand what changed its worth." Swift came the reply:

"The touch of the master's hand."

And many a man with life out of tune, and battered and scarred with sin,

Is auctioned cheap to the thoughtless crowd,

Much like that old violin.

A "mess of pottage," a glass of wine, a game, and he travels on.

He's "going" once, and "going" twice, he's "going" and almost "gone."

But the Master comes, and the foolish crowd never can quite understand

The worth of a soul and the change that's been wrought

By the touch of the master's hand.

— Myra Brook Welch

At this very moment, you might be in the presence of greatness, yet you could be overlooking it because you're distracted by thoughts of limitation. Your friends, co-workers, or family members may be talented souls with extraordinary gifts, but if you're paying attention to what's wrong with them, their beauty will escape you and waste away. Then you'll find yourself wondering why people are so disappointing and life always lets you down. Meanwhile, the vast riches in your life are going unnoticed and remain untapped.

Sometimes you might encounter great beings while they're passing through a dark night of the soul. As you observe them in the midst of their ordeal, you might not think much of them. But if you peer beyond their dilemma and recognize the genius within them, you'll see through the eyes of God, and you'll hasten their renaissance.

When you love and believe in someone (including yourself), you call forth their magnificence. Regard your loved ones with higher vision, and they'll fulfill it. As Dale Carnegie implored: "Give them a reputation to live up to!" Never give up on a person or project, for nothing is washed up unless you believe it is. There's a spark of life in all things, and as you acknowledge it, you can resurrect the supposed dead.

Likewise, *you* are a master in the making. Your potential is far more than you've exercised. You can draw it forth by focusing on your strengths rather than your weaknesses. Quit rehashing where you came from, and get excited about where you want to go. Are you willing to allow your true power to emerge?

God has never given up on you and never will. God sees you as you hope you are, not as you fear you are. Extend the same faith to those you encounter—beginning with yourself—and miracles will unfold before you.

The Path with Heart

All paths are the same; they lead nowhere. . . . In my own life, I could say I have traversed long, long paths, but I am not anywhere. My benefactor's question has meaning now. Does this path have a heart? If it does, the path is good; if it doesn't, it is of no use. Both paths lead nowhere; but one has a heart, the other doesn't. One makes for a joyful journey; as long as you follow it, you are one with it. The other will make you curse your life. One makes you strong; the other weakens you.

— from *The Teachings of Don Juan: A Yaqui Way of Knowledge*, by Carlos Castaneda

You have a path that matches your spirit. To know if the path you're on is the right one, consult your heart. If you feel alive and fulfilled, you can be certain that you're on your right course. However, if your heart is empty, hungry, or conflicted, look deeper . . . your spirit is trying to tell you something.

So many people have settled for the path without heart that it seems normal—*but it isn't natural.* Others may try to convince you that you're being naïve or that it's impossible to live your dream. It isn't. In fact, soul satisfaction is the only goal that will ever bring you true peace. It's the purpose for which you live.

Never give up on following your truth. Don't compromise on what you know is real. When you accept that you're here to be happy, your life will transform and your heart will be full. Then, when you come to the end of your journey, you'll be able to say, "Well done."

YOUR SACRED DUTY

Men of the earth, brothers in eternity, shake your souls awake! The hour long waited for, the promised hour has come. Over the dark firmament of suffering is rising the morning star heralding the day when you will understand that man's most sacred duty is to be man. That is to manifest life, intelligence, truth, and love. There is no higher aim, no vaster problem, and you who realize this will break the fetters with which ignorance and fear have bound unconscious humanity and will stand up free and know yourselves to be the eternal manifestation of the unmanifest witnesses of the absolute sons of that great All whom you call God.

— Found inscribed in a Russian church,
circa World War I

You weren't born to suffer; you were born to shine. Although love is our nature and joy is our purpose, many people instead accept struggle as a way of life. This was never the Creator's intention for you or anyone. God intends for you to be fully alive and celebrate all the gifts in and around you.

Turmoil is a call for awakening. Every challenge, great or small, is moving you to look deeper and draw forth the highest in you. You're never given a challenge beyond your ability to meet and master. You'll rise above every circumstance because you're greater than any circumstance.

We're all offspring and expressions of God. Something inside you is eternally connected to your Creator. Nothing that happens during the course of your worldly adventure can remove that union. No pain, fear, sin, or death can sever your bond to the Source of all things, your identity with It, and your purpose as an extension of It.

Act with the dignity and license of a higher order of being. You'll be affirmed and supported. You're not here to fix anything or prove yourself; you're here to be all that you are and shine your true nature into life.

References

Many of the stories and quotes included in this book are part of an oral tradition passed down through generations of storytellers, ministers, teachers, and lecturers, and, more recently, the Internet. As such, the original source of such material is unknown, and is believed to be in the public domain. The author has made every effort to ascertain and properly credit sources of copyrighted material. If you're aware of authorship or copyright of any material in this book that isn't listed or is improperly listed, please contact the author at the address in the back of this book so that proper acknowledgment can be made in future printings.

Below are credits for material for which copyright is known:

15—Your Inner Bible: Theophane the Monk, *Tales of a Magic Monastery*, © 1981 Crossroad. Used by permission. All rights reserved.

17—Relief and Release: Glenn Van Ekeren, *12 Simple Secrets of Happiness: Finding Joy in Everyday Relationships*, © 2000

Prentice Hall. Used by permission. All rights reserved.

23—Trust Your Instincts: *Bonkers!* magazine

25—The Best News: Arthur Lenehan, as cited in *The Best of Bits and Pieces,* © 1994 Ragan Communications. Used by permission. All rights reserved.

31—True Compassion: Parker J. Palmer, *The Active Life: A Spirituality of Work, Creativity, and Caring,* © 1990 HarperCollins. Used by permission. All rights reserved.

33—Reach into Majesty: Coleman Barks and John Moyne, *The Essential Rumi,* © 1995 HarperCollins. Used by permission. All rights reserved.

51—The Path with Heart: Carlos Castaneda, *The Teachings of Don Juan: A Yaqui Way of Knowledge, 30th Anniversary Edition,* © 1968 Regents of the University of California; © renewed 1996 by Carlos Casteneda. Used by permission. All rights reserved.

About the Author

Alan Cohen is the author of 20 popular inspirational books, including the best-selling *The Dragon Doesn't Live Here Anymore* and the award-winning *A Deep Breath of Life.* Alan is a contributing writer for the *New York Times* #1 bestselling *Chicken Soup for the Soul* series, and his books have been translated into 14 languages.

Each month Alan's column, "From the Heart," is published in numerous magazines internationally. His interviews and articles have been celebrated in *New Realities, New Woman, First for Women, Science of Mind, Unity, Personal Transformation, Human Potential,* and *Visions* magazines.

A frequent guest on radio and television, Alan has appeared on CNN, FOX, CNBC, and many *Good Morning* shows throughout the nation. His presentations are regularly broadcast via satellite on the Wisdom Channel, and he is a faculty member at Omega Institute for Holistic Studies in New York. Alan also guides groups on excursions to sacred sites such as Machu Picchu, Bali, and Egypt.

Alan resides in Maui, Hawaii, where he conducts retreats in visionary living.

For information on Alan Cohen's books, tapes, Hawaii retreats, journeys to sacred sites, on-line prosperity course, or seminars in your area:

Visit: **www.alancohen.com**
E-mail: admin@alancohen.com
Phone: 800-568-3079
Fax: 808-572-1023
or write to:
Alan Cohen Programs and Publications
455A Kukuna Road
Haiku, HI 96708

Also by Alan Cohen

Books

Are You as Happy as Your Dog?

Dare to Be Yourself

A Deep Breath of Life

The Dragon Doesn't Live Here Anymore

Handle With Prayer

Happily Even After

Have You Hugged a Monster Today?

I Had It All the Time

Joy Is My Compass

Lifestyles of the Rich in Spirit

Looking in for Number One

My Father's Voice

The Peace that You Seek

Rising in Love

Setting the Seen

Why Your Life Sucks and What You Can Do about It

(*Also available as an audio book)

Audios

Deep Relaxation

Eden Morning

I Believe in You

Journey to the Center of the Heart (also on CD)

Living from the Heart

Peace

We hope you enjoyed this Hay House Lifestyles book.
If you would like to receive a free catalog featuring additional Hay House books and products, or if you would like information about the Hay Foundation, please contact:

Hay House, Inc.
P.O. Box 5100
Carlsbad, CA 92018-5100

(760) 431-7695 or (800) 654-5126
(760) 431-6948 (fax) or (800) 650-5115 (fax)
www.hayhouse.com

Published and distributed in Australia by:
Hay House Australia Pty Ltd, P.O. Box 515,
Brighton-Le-Sands, NSW 2216
phone: 1800 023 516 • e-mail: info@hayhouse.com.au

Distributed in the United Kingdom by:
Airlift, 8 The Arena, Mollison Ave.,
Enfield, Middlesex, United Kingdom EN3 7NL

Distributed in Canada by:
Raincoast, 9050 Shaughnessy St.,
Vancouver, B.C., Canada V6P 6